Man

and

Nature

Sri Mata Amritanandamayi Devi

Man and Nature

by Sri Mata Amritanandamayi
Translated from Malayalam by Swami Amritaswarupananda

Published by
Mata Amritanandamayi Mission Trust
Amritapuri P. O., Kollam Dist.,
Kerala 690 525, India
Email: info@theammashop.org
Website: www.amritapuri.org

First Edition 1994
Printed 1994 - 2007: 20,000 copies
Tenth Edition 2008: 1,000 copies

Layout at Amrita DTP

Copyright © 2000 by Mata Amritanandamayi Center.

All rights reserved. No part of this publication may be stored in a retrieval system, transmitted, reproduced, transcribed or translated into any language, in any form, by any means without the prior agreement and written permission of the publisher.

❀

*"Only through love and compassion
is the protection and preservation
of Nature possible."*

Preface

Life teaches us that experience is the best form of education. Real Teachers are those who awaken the knowledge which already exists within us, and who remind us that knowing something and yet, not doing anything about it, is the same as not knowing. Mother's inimitable way of transforming our knowing into doing, arises from Her loving reminder that "Religion is something to be lived."

Religion is an attempt to erase our false perception of the ego and to remove the sense of duality from our lives, that artificial distinction between the ego and everything else. The same sense of ego that stops us from being

compassionate towards other human beings, because we mistakenly believe ourselves to be separate, also allows us to destroy the environment because we do not realize that we are part of it. Most people still act as if the environment is some place, far away in the forests or the mountains, rather than the place where we all live, or the beings that we are. Mother says that "To deny the existence of God is to deny one's own existence." So it is with Nature, which is God in visible form. Although many people believe that man was meant to conquer Nature, in attempting to do so we have become our own worst enemy. We are a part of Nature. Her continued capacity to protect and nurture depends on our ability to re-establish a balance in our relation to the Earth and all its creatures.

Mother's words are an appeal to discover the quiet selflessness which slumbers within all of us. Nature is also calling. But Her cries have become more strident of late, as humans are destroying more and more of Earth's capacity for renewal. Being part of Nature means that we ourselves are the environment. We must begin to see that the Earth's needs are exactly the same as our own.

Preface

There is nothing to add to Mother's discussion on Nature and our role on this planet. This is hardly surprising given the indivisibility between God and Nature, for indeed they are one and the same. To deny Nature diminishes our own spirit and our capacity for freedom. The same stillness that we seek within is the same stillness that still pervades the forests, the oceans and mountain tops. And in the same way that we must focus and strive to still our inner turmoil and find peace, we must also act to undo the damage which we wreak against Nature. Service to the Earth and its creatures is no less a service to God than any other form of service. Let us renew our faith in service to the Earth.

—Sam La Budde
Director
Endangered Species Project

Contents

Question: What is the relationship between man and Nature? 10

Question: What part does religion play in the relationship between man and Nature? 12

Question: What caused the break in the relationship between Nature and human beings? 22

Question: What is the connection between spiritual practices and the protection of Nature? 27

Question: How serious is the environmental problem? 32

Question: Are human beings becoming a threat to the very existence of life on earth? 39

Question: Is it necessary to give more importance to human needs than to Nature? 40

Question: What are the steps that can be taken in societyto prevent the destruction of Nature and animals? 41

Question: Are the forests an indispensable part of the earth? 44

Question: Is it advisable to approach spiritual masters without trying to solve the current problems ourselves? 45

MAN AND NATURE

Earth Island Institute
San Francisco, CA

The following are Mother's answers to questions on environmental issues presented to Her by Mr. Sam La Budde, a leading environmentalist in the United States.

Question: What is the relationship between man and Nature?

AMMA: Children, man is not different from Nature. He is part of Nature. The very existence of human beings on earth depends on Nature. In truth, we are not protecting Nature — it is Nature who protects us. Trees and plants, for example, are absolutely necessary for the purification of vital energy (the life force). Everyone knows that human beings cannot live in a desert. The reason is that there are no trees there to purify the vital energy. If atmospheric purification does not take place, the health of humans will deteriorate. It will cause a decrease in their life span, various diseases, and poor eyesight or even blindness. Our lives are inextricably dependent on Nature; even a small change in Nature

Interview with Amma

will affect our lives on this planet. Similarly, man's thoughts and actions have an effect on Nature. If the balance in Nature is lost, the harmony of human life will also be lost, and vice versa.

The one factor which connects a human being to Nature is the innate innocence within man. When we see a rainbow, or the waves of the ocean, do we still feel the innocent joy of a child? An adult who experiences a rainbow as being nothing but light waves will not know the joy and wonder of a child who sees a rainbow, or a child who is watching the waves of the ocean.

Faith in God is the best way to sustain this childlike innocence in man. He who has faith and devotion to God, which in turn stems from his innate innocence, beholds God in everything, in every tree and animal, in every aspect of Nature. This attitude enables him to live in perfect harmony, in tune with Nature. The never ending stream of love that flows from a true believer towards the entire Creation will have a gentle, soothing effect on Nature. This love is the best protection of Nature.

It is when our selfishness increases that we

begin to lose our innocence. When this happens, man becomes estranged from Nature and begins to exploit her. Man doesn't know what a terrible threat he has become to her. By harming Nature, he is paving the way for his own destruction.

As man's intellect and scientific knowledge grow, he should not forget the feelings of his heart, which enable him to live in accordance with Nature and her fundamental laws.

Question: What part does religion play in the relationship between man and Nature?

MMA: It is religion that helps a person to maintain the awareness that he or she is not separate from Nature. Without religion mankind loses that awareness. Religion teaches us to love Nature. In truth, the progress and prosperity of mankind depend solely on the good which man does for Nature. Religion helps to maintain a harmonious relationship between human beings, between the individual and society, and between man and Nature.

The relationship between man and Nature is like the relationship between Pindanada

Interview with Amma

> *By establishing a loving relationship between man and Nature, they ensured both the balance of Nature and the progress of the human race.*

(the microcosm) and Brahmananda (the macrocosm). Our great ancestors understood this. That is why they gave so much importance to Nature worship in religious practices. The idea behind all religious *acharam* (practices) was to closely associate human beings with Nature. By establishing a loving relationship between man and Nature, they ensured both the balance of Nature and the progress of the human race.

Look at a tree. It gives shade even to the person who cuts it down. It gives its sweet, delicious fruits to the person who harms it. But our attitude is completely different. When we plant a tree, or raise an animal, we are only concerned about the profit we will make from it. If the animal ceases to make a profit, we will have it destroyed without delay. As soon as the cow stops

producing milk, we will sell it to the butcher in order to make money. If a tree stops yielding fruit, we will cut it down and make furniture or something else from it. Selfishness reigns supreme. Selfless love cannot be found anywhere. But our ancestors were not like this. They knew that trees, plants and animals were absolutely necessary for the benefit and good of humans. They foresaw that man, in his selfish moments, would forget Nature, and would cease to have any concern for her. They also knew that future generations would suffer, due to man's disassociation from Nature. They therefore linked each religious rite with Nature. Thus, through religious principles, they could succeed in developing an emotional bond between man and Nature. The Ancients loved and worshipped trees and plants, such as the banyan tree, bilva and tulasi, not because the trees bore fruit and helped them to make a profit, but because the Ancients knew that they themselves in truth were one with all of Nature.

Religion teaches man to love the entire

Interview with Amma

Creation. Some people mock religion saying that it is mere blind belief; yet it is generally found that the actions of such people do greater harm to Nature than those who believe in God. It is the religious minded people, not these so-called intellectuals, who protect, preserve and love Nature. There are some people who, by quoting modern scientific theories, are always trying to prove that whatever religion teaches is wrong. The truth is that the reverence and devotion that human beings develop through their religious faith are always beneficial, both to humanity and to Nature.

Religion teaches us to worship God within Nature. Through the stories of Sri Krishna's life, the tulasi (basil) plant and the cow have become very dear to the people of India, who lovingly protect and look after them. In times past, there would be a pond and a small grove of trees adjoining every house in India. Each home had a tulasi plant growing in the front yard. Tulasi leaves are highly medicinal. The leaves won't decay, even if plucked and kept for several days; the medicinal potency remains. Part of the daily routine in those days was to water the tulasi

plant every morning, bowing down with reverence and devotion in front of it, worshipping it as an embodiment of the Goddess. This was the traditional way of reverence and worship which the Indians also showed to other trees, such as the banyan, the bilva and the fig. The medicinal value of tulasi leaves, which was known to the ancients rishis eons ago, has now been proven through modern scientific experiments. But the question is, do scientists and others who have discovered the medicinal value of the tulasi and other sacred plants, show the same love and reverence toward Nature as the Ancients did, who were inspired by their religious faith? Is it not religious faith which helps to protect and preserve Nature, rather than the knowledge obtained through modern science?

Suppose you have ten seeds. Consume nine of them if you want, but let at least one seed remain for planting. Nothing should be destroyed completely. If you receive a hundred dollars from a harvest, at least ten dollars should be given to charity.

The scriptures of India teach that a householder should perform the *pancha yajnas,* or five

Interview with Amma

daily sacrifices. The first of these is the *deva yajna,* or worshipping of God, the Supreme Power, which is to be done with devotion and to the best of one's ability. Next comes *rishi yajna,* or the adoration of the sages. The ancient God-Realized sages did not allow their unique experiences to vanish into oblivion. Out of compassion for humanity, they passed them on in the form of scriptures and other sacred writings. A devout study and practice of the scriptural teachings

constitute this sacrifice. The third is *pitru yajna.* This consists of showing respect and rendering service towards one's parents and elders. It also includes thinking holy and auspicious thoughts for the welfare of one's departed ancestors. Fourth comes *nara yajna,* or service rendered to mankind. This includes all forms of selfless service, such as feeding the poor and serving the sick and the aged. *Bhuta yajna* is the last sacrifice; it is to serve all living beings as embodiments of

Man and Nature

the Universal Being. This is done through the feeding of and caring for the animal kingdom and the plants. In olden days family members never ate before feeding their domestic birds and animals. They would also water their plants and trees before eating. In those days, worshipping Nature and natural phenomenon were part and parcel of human life. People were always eager to please Nature in gratitude for her kind gifts. *Bhuta yajna* brings about the consciousness of the unity of all life. Through these rituals and sacrifices, human beings learn to live in harmony with society and Nature.

More than the knowledge of modern science, it is the deeper understanding of religion, the truth of the oneness of all Creation, which teaches humans to love Nature, and to develop a sense of reverence and devotion to all. The love that religion teaches is not the kind of love which a gross intellect can understand. It is that of the heart. It can only be imbibed by a person who is endowed with a subtle intellect born out of faith.

If there is a policeman in a village, fewer thefts will occur because people fear him. Similarly, reverence and devotion to God help to

Interview with Amma

maintain *dharma,* or right conduct, in society. By truly imbibing the principles of religion, and by observing the prescribed customs, people can avoid committing mistakes.

Those who declare that religion is merely a collection of blind beliefs will not spare even

a moment in order to try to understand the scientific principles behind religious practices. Modern science can produce rain by spraying silver iodide in the clouds. However, the water from such unnaturally caused rain may not be completely pure. The scriptures, on the other hand, prescribe certain ritual sacrifices that will bring rain. The wise ones know that the purity of rain water obtained through these means is far superior to water obtained through unnatural methods, such as cloud seeding.

In a similar manner, a very beneficial change both for Nature and for human beings can be brought about by offering prescribed ingredients into the sacrificial fire. All such sacrifices and rituals help to restore the lost harmony and balance of Nature. Just as ayurvedic herbs and plants cure physical diseases, the smoke that emanates from the sacrificial fire, in which ingredients of medicinal value are offered, purifies the atmosphere. Burning incense, lighting oil lamps, offering pure food in a sacrificial fire, or to God, also helps cleanse the atmosphere. The side effects of such rituals will not create as much pollution as chlorine and the disinfectants which

Interview with Amma

are used for purifying water and destroying germs. The smoke that comes from the sacrificial fire also helps to cleanse the respiratory system, by removing the mucus and phlegm that block the air passages.

Modern science says that it is harmful to look directly at the sun during a solar eclipse. The same cautionary advice was given by the ancient rishis eons ago. Using a primitive but effective method, they only looked at the sun's image reflected in water, in which cow dung had been dissolved.

By protecting and preserving wild and domestic animals, trees and plants, we are protecting and preserving Nature. The Ancients worshipped the cow and the earth, including them amongst the five mothers (*pancha matas*). The five mothers were: *dehamata* — the biological mother, *desamata* — the motherland, *bhumata* — Mother Earth, *vedamata* — the Vedas, and *gomata* — the cow. To our ancestors, the cow was not just a four legged creature, but a sacred animal which was worshipped as a form of the Mother (the Goddess).

No religion can exist disassociated from Nature. Religion is the link that binds mankind to Nature. Religion removes the ego in man, enabling him to know and experience his oneness with Nature.

Question: What caused the break in the relationship between Nature and human beings?

MMA: Because of his selfishness, man today sees Nature as being separate from himself. If a person receives a cut or a wound, it is certainly the awareness that both the left and right hand are "mine" that prompts the

Interview with Amma

one to comfort the other. We don't have the same concern when an injury happens to someone else, do we? This is because of the attitude that "It is not mine". The wall of separation between humans and Nature is created mainly by the selfish attitude of humans. They think that Nature has been created only for them to use and exploit in order to fulfill their selfish desires. This attitude creates a wall, a separation and a distance. It is a frightening truth that modern man has lost his broad-mindedness as a result of the tremendous growth of modern science. Man has found methods to produce a hundred tomatoes from a plant that could otherwise bear only ten fruits. He has also succeeded in doubling their size. While it is true that due to increased production, poverty and starvation have been reduced to a certain extent, man is not very aware of the harmful effects caused by artificial fertilizers and pesticides, which get into his body through the food that he eats. But it is also a fact that such chemicals destroy the cells of the body and make him an easy victim of disease. The number of hospitals have also had to increase, as scientist artificially force plants to yield fruit and

seeds in quantities which are far beyond their limits. Science has reached unimaginable heights, but owing to his selfishness, man has lost the clarity to see the truth of things and to act with discrimination.

It is the selfish thought of wanting more that prompts man to use artificial fertilizers and pesticides. It is because of his greed that he does not care to love the plants. A balloon can be inflated only up to a limit. After that it will burst if you keep blowing air into it. Likewise, a seed has a certain limit to the yield it can give. Without taking this into account, if we keep on trying to increase the production by the use of artificial means, it will badly affect the strength and quality of the seed. It also does harm to those who eat it. In olden days only water and natural manure were sufficient for cultivation. But today the

Interview with Amma

situation is different. Pesticides and fertilizers have become part and parcel of farming. So much so, that the immune systems of plants and seeds have become very weak, and have lost their power to fight disease. Through natural methods we can strengthen their power to resist disease. Religion tells us to humbly love everything with reverence. Scientific inventions have managed to vastly increase our production, but at the same time, the quality of everything has decreased.

To cage a bird or an animal is just like putting a human being behind bars. Freedom is the birth right of every living being. Who are we to take that freedom away? By injecting hormones into a hen, we try to make the size of the eggs bigger. We make hens lay two eggs a day, by shutting them in dark cubicles which are opened periodically, in order to create a false impression in the hen that one more day has passed. But by doing so, the hen's life span is shortened by half, and the eggs lose all their quality. The thought of profit has made man blind and destroyed all his goodness and virtues. This does not mean that we shouldn't think about increasing production. Not at all. The point is that there is a limit to

MAN AND NATURE

everything, and crossing that limit is equal to destroying Nature.

It is high time to give serious thought to protecting Nature. The destruction of Nature is the same thing as the destruction of humanity. Trees, animals, birds, plants, forests, mountains, lakes and rivers — everything that exists in Nature — are in desperate need of our kindness, of the compassionate care and protection of man. If we protect them, they, in turn, will protect us.

The legendary dinosaur and many other living species have been completely wiped out from the face of the earth, because they could not live in the changing climatic conditions. In a similar manner, if man is not careful, when his

Interview with Amma

selfishness has reached its peak, he too will have to succumb to the same fate.

Only through love and compassion is the protection and preservation of Nature possible. But both these qualities are fast diminishing in human beings. In order to feel real love and compassion, one must realize the oneness of the life force that sustains and is the substratum of the entire universe. This realization can only be attained through a deep study of religion and the observance of spiritual principles.

Question: What is the connection between spiritual practices and the protection of Nature?

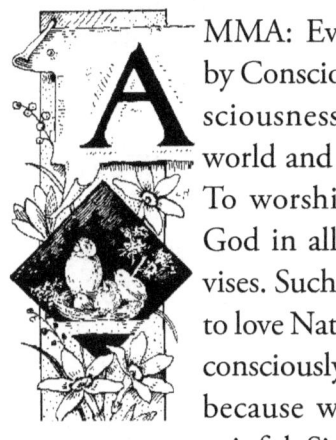

AMMA: Everything is pervaded by Consciousness. It is that Consciousness which sustains the world and all the creatures in it. To worship everything, seeing God in all, is what religion advises. Such an attitude teaches us to love Nature. None of us would consciously injure our own body, because we know it would be painful. Similarly, we will feel the

Man and Nature

pain of other people to be our own when the realization dawns within us that everything is pervaded by one and the same Consciousness. Compassion will arise, and we will sincerely wish to help and protect all. In that state, we won't feel like plucking even a leaf unnecessarily. We will pick a flower only on the last day of its existence, before it falls from the stem. We will consider it as very harmful to the plant, and to Nature, if the flower is plucked on its very first day due to our greediness.

In days gone by, every house had a family shrine room. People used to grow flowers in the yard surrounding the house. Devoted care would be given to the garden. The flowers from those plants which were planted and grown with loving care by the family were offered to God during worship.

Whatever is provided by Nature, the very source of flowers and plants, should be lovingly returned

Interview with Amma

to it. This is the symbolism behind the offering of flowers to God. It also helps to enhance our devotion to God. Worship performed with one-pointedness helps to diminish thoughts, and this in turn will cleanse and purify the mind.

Some years ago, the garden or surrounding land of each home contained a wood or a tree grove, with a small temple. The wood or grove contained highly medicinal trees such as the banyan, fig, and bilva (wood apple). The shrine and the wood was the common worship place of the

entire family. At dusk the family used to gather at the shrine to chant the divine Names and offer their prayers in front of lighted oil lamps. Modern science has recently discovered that music will enhance the healthy growth of plants and trees. Besides the bliss that devotional singing gives to all creatures, if it is done with love, it bestows purity and peace to our minds. The

wind that filters through the leaves of medicinal trees and plants is also good for our health. The smoke from both the oil-soaked wick burning in the brass lamp and the pure bee wax candle will kill the germs in the atmosphere. But over and above all, prayers done with concentration will restore the lost harmony of Nature.

If an ordinary person can be compared to an electric lamp, a real sadhak (spiritual aspirant) can be compared to a transformer. By making the mind still and conserving energy, which otherwise would be dissipated through overindulgence and pleasure seeking, the *sadhak* awakens the infinite source of power within him. Having no likes or dislikes himself, even his breath becomes beneficial to Nature. Just as water is purified by a filter, the *prana* (vital force) of the *tapasvi* (ascetic) is a filter which purifies Nature. Ayurvedic physicians will use a certain natural stone to purify the oil that has been boiled with medicinal herbs, in the preparation of some

Interview with Amma

remedies. Likewise, the *tapasvi's* pure vital energy can purify Nature by correcting the imbalances created by man.

Looking at Nature and observing its selfless way of giving, we can become aware of our own limitations. That will help to develop devotion and self-surrender to God. Thus, Nature helps us to become closer to God and teaches us to truly worship Him. In reality, Nature is nothing but God's visible form which we can behold and experience through our senses. Indeed, by loving and serving Nature, we are worshipping God Himself.

Just as Nature creates the favorable circumstances for a coconut to become a coconut tree, and for a seed to transform itself into a huge fruit tree, Nature creates the necessary circumstances through which the individual soul can reach the Supreme Being and merge in eternal union with Him.

A sincere Truth seeker, or a true believer, cannot harm Nature because he or she sees Nature as God — he doesn't experience Nature as being separate from himself. He is the real lover of Nature.

 Man and Nature

Mother would say that a real scientist should be a real lover — a lover of mankind, a lover of all creation and a lover of life.

Question: How serious is the environmental problem?

 MMA: In days gone by, there was a fixed time for everything. It was the practice to do cultivation during a certain month or season, and a particular month was fixed for harvesting. There were no deep tube wells

in those days. The farmers depended solely on the water and sunshine which was graciously bestowed by Nature. The people lived in harmony with Nature. They never tried to challenge Nature. Nature was therefore always helpful to man. Nature was his friend. People were completely confident that it would rain if the seeds were sown during a particular time of the month.

Interview with Amma

They also knew the exact time when the crop would be ready for harvest. Everything went smoothly. Nature bestowed both rain and sunshine at the right time, without fail. Excessive or untimely rain never destroyed the crops, nor was there any excess or lack of sunshine. Everything was balanced. Human beings never tried to act against the laws of Nature. Mutual understanding, faith, love, compassion and cooperation existed among people. They loved and worshipped Nature, and in return Nature blessed them with an abundance of natural wealth. Such an attitude alone will help to uplift society as a whole. But things have changed.

Scientific inventions are highly beneficial. But they should not be against Nature. The constant harm done by human beings has destroyed Nature's patience. She has begun to retaliate. Natural calamities are greatly increasing. Nature has commenced Her dance of final dissolution. She has lost Her balance owing to the unrighteous actions perpetrated against Her by humans. This is the main cause of all the suffering that human beings are undergoing during this present age.

The scientist who is inventive and who

experiments may have love within him. But that love is limited to a narrow channel. It is directed only to the scientific field in which he works. It doesn't embrace all creation. He is more or less bound to the laboratory where he sits, or to the scientific equipment which he uses. He does not think of real life. He is more interested in finding out whether there is life on the moon or on Mars. He is more interested in inventing nuclear armaments.

A scientist may claim he is trying to find the truth of the empirical world

Interview with Amma

through an analytic approach. He dissects things in order to analyze how they function. If he is given a kitten, he is more interested in using the animal for research than in loving it as a pet. He will measure its rate of breathing, its pulse and blood pressure. In the name of science and the search for truth, he will dissect the animal and examine its organs. Once the kitten has been cut open, it is dead. Life disappears and any possibility for love is gone. Only if there is life is there love. In his search for the truth of life, the scientist unwittingly destroys life itself. Strange!

A rishi is a real lover because he has dived into his own Self, the very core of life and love. He experiences life and love everywhere — above, below, in front, behind — in all direction. Even in hell, even in the nether world, he sees nothing but life and love. For him there is nothing but life and love shining forth with splendor and glory from all directions. Therefore, Mother would say he is 'a real scientist'. He experiments in the inner laboratory of his own being. He never creates division in life. For him life is one whole. He always dwells in that undivided state of love and life.

The real scientist, the sage, lovingly embraces life and becomes one with it. He never tries to fight with life. While the scientist tries to fight and conquer life, the sage simply surrenders to life and lets it carry him wherever it may.

Man has turned against Nature. Man no longer cares about Nature. He is more interested in exploring and experimenting. He is trying to break all bounds. But he does not know that by doing so, he is paving the way for his own

Interview with Amma

destruction. It is like lying on one's back and spitting up. The spittle will fall on one's own face.

Today, in addition to the exploitation of Nature, humans are also polluting her. There was a time when cow dung was used as a disinfectant in India, when children were given their vaccinations. But now, a wound would become septic and the person would die if cow dung were to be applied. The substance that used to be a medicine that healed the wound has now turned into something that causes infection. So much poison must have gone into the cow dung through the grass, hay and oil cakes with which we feed the cows.

Now there is no longer any rain when it is supposed to rain. If it does rain, there is either too little or too much, and it comes too early or too late. It is the same with sunshine. Nowadays humans are trying to exploit Nature. This is why there are floods, droughts and earthquakes, and everything is being destroyed.

There is a tremendous decline in the quality of life. Many people have lost faith. They do not feel any love and compassion, and the team spirit of working together, hand in hand, for the good

Man and Nature

of all, has been lost. This will have a bad effect on Nature. Nature will withdraw all her blessings and turn against man. Unimaginable will be Nature's reaction if man continues like this.

There is a story about a couple who had a liquor shop. The husband always told his wife, "Pray to God that He will bring us more customers." The wife sincerely obeyed her husband's words. One day, one of their customers noticed that she was praying, and said to her, "Please pray for me also, so that I will get more work". What is your job?" asked the wife. "I am a coffin maker," said the man.

This is the present state of the world. It has become a world in which people are only concerned about their own interests.

Interview with Amma

Question: Are human beings becoming a threat to the very existence of life on earth?

AMMA: When Nature graciously protects and serves human beings, it is, without question, their responsibility to return that protection and service to Nature. Modern science says that trees and plants can respond in an imperceptible way to the thoughts and actions of human beings. Science has discovered that plants tremble with fear when we go near them with the intention of plucking their leaves. But ages ago, the saints and sages of India, having understood this great truth, lived a life of complete harmlessness.

There is a story in the Hindu scriptures, called Sakunthalam, which demonstrates this point. Once a sage found an abandoned child in a forest. He brought the child to his hermitage and raised her there as his own. When she grew up, the sage entrusted her with the job of looking after the plants and domestic animals of the hermitage. She loved the plants and animals as much as her own life. One day when the sage

was away, the king who ruled that country saw this beautiful girl, while riding through the forest during a hunting expedition. He fell in love with her and desired to marry her. On his return, the sage came to know about it and gladly consented to the king's wish. After the marriage ceremony, the girl was about to leave the hermitage for the king's palace. At that time the jasmine plant which she had always loved and carefully tended bent down and coiled softly around her ankles. The animals shed tears when she left. This illustrates how plants, trees and all of Nature will return our love if we really care about them.

Question: Is it necessary to give more importance to human needs than to Nature?

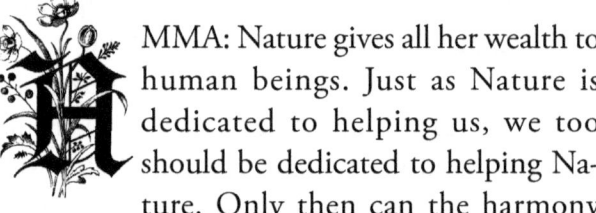

MMA: Nature gives all her wealth to human beings. Just as Nature is dedicated to helping us, we too should be dedicated to helping Nature. Only then can the harmony between Nature and human beings be preserved. To pluck ten leaves, when only five leaves are sufficient, is a sin. Suppose two potatoes are enough to cook a dish. If you take a third

Interview with Amma

potato, you are acting indiscriminately — you are committing an *adharmic* (unrighteous) act.

Using Nature for our needs cannot be considered wrong. But exploitation changes the whole set of circumstances. This makes our action an unrighteous one. First of all, we are unnecessarily destroying the life of the extra plant, animal or whatever it is that we exploit. Secondly, we deny it for someone else's use. Someone else could have used it, perhaps our neighbor who does not have anything to eat. Thus, when we exploit Nature, we are exploiting others. It is certainly a necessity to have a house to protect us from the rain and the sun. But we should not build a house in order to make a show of our wealth and luxurious life style. Cutting down enough trees to build a house cannot be considered to be unrighteous. An act becomes unrighteous or sinful when we perform it indiscriminately, without any alertness. Spending lavishly without thinking of God, the Great Giver, or the others who would be benefited by the extra money — that is unrighteousness.

Question: What are the steps that can be taken

in society to prevent the destruction of Nature and animals?

MMA: It is certainly high time to take stern steps to prevent man from destroying Nature and the resources which she kindly bestows on us, as a gift or reward for the good actions we perform. The implementation of strict rules would be beneficial; but there is a need for people who are prepared to obey and execute such rules. Nowadays, those who are supposed to observe the rules are the first to break them. Societies should be formed in each and every village, in order to create an awareness of the significance of protecting and preserving Nature. Mere intellectual understanding is not enough. People should be taught to function from their hearts. The teachers and counselors of these societies should have the ability to encourage people to love Nature, to feel compassion for all of Creation and its creatures. The teachers and counselors themselves should be highly competent and efficient people, who can inspire others to do whatever they are taught. Only then will

Interview with Amma

there be any benefit. The support of religion and spiritual principles will greatly help to achieve this goal.

A major cause of pollution in the atmosphere is the toxic smoke which emanates from huge machines in factories and other industries. This affects the healthy growth of plants and trees. The toxins produced from such places also badly damage the health of humans. Necessary steps should be taken to protect and preserve the trees and plants, which grow in the areas surrounding the factories and other industrial sites. In fact, it is these trees and plants which, to a great extent, cleanse and purify the polluted atmosphere of such places. But for the existence of these plants, the situation would be much worse. The initiative to preserve the natural surroundings should come from the entrepreneurs and employees of such companies.

A government alone cannot do anything without the sincere and wholehearted cooperation of the people. For this to happen, it should be a government which works in accordance with the will and wishes of the people who love Nature. This again demands support from political leaders and government officials. They should not just be a group of people who are craving money and position. Their aim should be the upliftment of the country and its people. A great deal will be achieved if they are people endowed with a selfless and universal outlook in their judgment.

Question: Are the forests an indispensable part of the earth?

MMA: Yes, very much so. Science is yet to understand the various benefits that the forests bestow on Nature. The Forests are part and parcel of the life on this planet. They are indispensable. They purify and prevent the overheating of the atmosphere, they keep the soil moist, they protect and preserve wildlife, etc.

In order to meet the necessities of life, it is not wrong to cut down trees and collect medicinal plants from the forests. But do not exploit and destroy the precious forests. Nature knows how to protect and take care of herself. At present we are exploiting Nature in the name of protection and preservation. Birds and animals

Interview with Amma

live happily in the forest. Man alone is their greatest enemy. By destroying Nature, man has become his own enemy. He knows not that he is digging his own grave when he brings down his axe on the foot of a tree.

Question: Is it advisable to approach spiritual masters without trying to solve the current problems ourselves?

AMMA: Experts can help you sort out many of the problems that you confront in your professional life. There is no doubt about it. But only God's power can make anything actually happen. In order for anything to happen, Grace is needed. Human effort, which is a product of the intellect, can only take us up to a certain point which it cannot cross. Beyond that point lies the realm of God's Grace. The fruition of our actions will not come to pass unless we manage to tap into that realm, which is beyond human reach. The best way to tap into that energy is by seeking the advice and blessings of a genuine spiritual Master. Such a great soul

MAN AND NATURE

Interview with Amma

is the very source of that Realm beyond. He or she is an inexhaustible source of power, the very embodiment of God's power and Grace. Experts can help, but cannot bless and bestow Grace. Even an expert's help may fail to bring about the right fruit, but a real spiritual Master's words and blessings will never fail.

Never look back and grieve. Look forward and smile. We should perform our actions with utmost faith and alertness, but with a sense of detachment. This is what the spiritual masters teach us. What is the use of feeling sad if a plant that we have grown withers away? Plant another one without brooding over the lost one. By brooding over the past, man becomes feeble-minded. This will cause the dissipation of all his energies.

A Master's mind is not like ours which runs only after the pleasures of the world. It is like a tree which gives shade and sweet fruits, even to those who cut it asunder. Although the sage burns away his life in selfless actions, like an incense stick which gives its fragrance to others at the cost of its own existence, he feels immense happiness in spreading love and peace to all of society. Only such a person can lead us, who

are full of ego and attachment, along the path of righteousness. Such sages are not meant for only one individual, class, creed or sect. They are meant for the whole world, for the entire human race.

Amritapuri, May 1994

Book Catalog
By Author

Sri Mata Amritanandamayi Devi
108 Quotes On Faith
108 Quotes On Love
Compassion, The Only Way To Peace: Paris Speech
Cultivating Strength And Vitality
Living In Harmony
May Peace And Happiness Prevail: Barcelona Speech
May Your Hearts Blossom: Chicago Speech
Practice Spiritual Values And Save The World: Delhi Speech
The Awakening Of Universal Motherhood: Geneva Speech
The Eternal Truth
The Infinite Potential Of Women: Jaipur Speech
Understanding And Collaboration Between Religions
Unity Is Peace: Interfaith Speech

Swami Amritaswarupananda Puri
Ammachi: A Biography
Awaken Children, Volumes 1-9
From Amma's Heart
Mother Of Sweet Bliss
The Color Of Rainbow

Swami Jnanamritananda Puri
Eternal Wisdom, Volumes 1-2

Swami Paramatmananda Puri
On The Road To Freedom Volumes 1-2
Talks, Volumes 1-6

Swami Purnamritananda Puri
Unforgettable Memories

Swami Ramakrishnananda Puri
Eye Of Wisdom
Racing Along The Razor's Edge
Secret Of Inner Peace
The Blessed Life
The Timeless Path
Ultimate Success

Swamini Krishnamrita Prana
Love Is The Answer
Sacred Journey
The Fragrance Of Pure Love
Torrential Love

M.A. Center Publications
1,000 Names Commentary
Archana Book (Large)
Archana Book (Small)
Being With Amma
Bhagavad Gita
Bhajanamritam, Volumes 1-6
Embracing The World
For My Children
Immortal Light
Lead Us To Purity
Lead Us To The Light
Man And Nature
My First Darshan
Puja: The Process Of Ritualistic Worship
Sri Lalitha Trishati Stotram

Amma's Websites

AMRITAPURI—Amma's Home Page
Teachings, Activities, Ashram Life, eServices, Yatra, Blogs and News
http://www.amritapuri.org

AMMA (Mata Amritanandamayi)
About Amma, Meeting Amma, Global Charities, Groups and Activities and Teachings
http://www.amma.org

EMBRACING THE WORLD®
Basic Needs, Emergencies, Environment, Research and News
http://www.embracingtheworld.org

AMRITA UNIVERSITY
About, Admissions, Campuses, Academics, Research, Global and News
http://www.amrita.edu

THE AMMA SHOP—Embracing the World® Books & Gifts Shop
Blog, Books, Complete Body, Home & Gifts, Jewelry, Music and Worship
http://www.theammashop.org

IAM—Integrated Amrita Meditation Technique®
Meditation Taught Free of Charge to the Public, Students, Prisoners and Military
http://www.amma.org/groups/north-america/projects/iam-meditation-classes

AMRITA PUJA
Types and Benefits of Pujas, Brahmasthanam Temple, Astrology Readings, Ordering Pujas
http://www.amritapuja.org

GREENFRIENDS
Growing Plants, Building Sustainable Environments, Education and Community Building
http://www.amma.org/groups/north-america/projects/green-friends

FACEBOOK
This is the Official Facebook Page to Connect with Amma
https://www.facebook.com/MataAmritanandamayi

DONATION PAGE
Please Help Support Amma's Charities Here:
http://www.amma.org/donations

www.ingramcontent.com/pod-product-compliance
Lightning Source LLC
Chambersburg PA
CBHW061345040426
42444CB00011B/3097